Information

a blue or black pen.

Start here

The Census must count every person living in the United States on April 1, 2010.

Before you answer Question 1, count the people living in this house, apartment, or mobile home using our guidelines.

- Count all people, including babies, who live and sleep here most of the time.

The Census Bureau also conducts counts in institutions and other places, so:

Do not count anyone living away either at college or in the Armed Forces.

Do not count anyone in a nursing home, jail, prison, detention facility, etc., on April 1, 2010.

~~people off your form, even if th~~

This is the official form for all the people at this addr~~ess~~ It is quick and easy, and your answers are protected by l~~aw~~

5. Please provide information for each person living here who owns or rent~~s this~~ home. If the owner or renter live~~s~~ living here. This will be Pers~~on 1~~ What is Person 1's nam~~e~~

Last Name

First Name

6. What is Person

☐ Male   ☐

7. What is P

Please rep~~ort~~

Age on Apri~~l~~

KAYE STEARMAN

This updated paperback edition
published in 2016
First published in 2011 by Wayland
Copyright © 2011 Wayland

Wayland
Carmelite House
50 Victoria Embankment
London EC4Y 0DZ

MIX
Paper from
responsible sources
FSC® C104740
www.fsc.org

Editor: Katie Woolley
Designer: Rita Storey

British Library Cataloguing in Publication
Data
 Stearman, Kaye.
   Freedom of information. -- (Ethical
   debates)
   1. Freedom of information--Juvenile
   literature.
   I. Title II. Series
   175-dc22

ISBN: 978 0 7502 9746 2
10 9 8 7 6 5 4 3 2 1
Printed in China

Wayland is a division of Hachette
Children's Group,
an Hachette UK company.
www.hachette.co.uk
Picture Acknowledgements:

Collection/TopFoto; P9 Alex Wong/Getty
Images; P10 Bettmann/Corbis;
P11 Sipa Press/Rex Features;
P12 Photoshot; P13 Shutterstock;
P14 Shutterstock; P16 Michael
Reynolds/epa/Corbis; P17Greg Allen/Rex
Features; P18 Shutterstock; P19 The Image
Works/TopFoto; P20 PA Photos/TopFoto;
P21; Karl-Josef Hildenbrand/dpa/Corbis;
P22 C3850 Andreas Gebert/dpa/Corbis;
P23 Shutterstock; P24 PA Photos/TopFoto;
P26 John Stillwell/Pool/epa/Corbis; P27
Hamad l Mohammed/Reuters/Corbis;
P29 Scott J Ferrell/Congressional
Quarterly/GettyImages; P30
Ullsteinbild/TopFoto; P31 AFP/Getty
Images; P32 Ocean/Corbis; P33 PA
Photos/TopFoto; P34 Shutterstock;
P35 Kevin Lamarque/Reuters/Corbis;
P37 TopFoto.co.uk; P38 Gireesh Gv/The
India Today Group/Getty Images;
P41 Rex Features; P42   Atta
Kenare/AFP/Getty Images; P43 Sia
Kambou/AFP/Getty Images; P44 Binod
Joshi/AP/Press Association Images

About the Consultant: Terry Fiehn worked
as a teacher, advisory teacher and teacher
trainer for over 20 years. He is co-author
of the *This is Citizenship* series of
textbooks and has written several history
textbooks and a wide range of educational
resources. He worked on the QCDA
Citizenship assessment working party
and monitoring programme.

Note: The website addresses (URLs) included in this book
were valid at the time of going to press. However, because of
the nature of the Internet, it is possible that some addresses
may have changed, or sites may have changed or closed
down since publication. While the author and publishers
regret any inconvenience this may cause to the readers, no
responsibility for any such changes can be accepted by either
the author or the publishers.

contents

Real-life case study

This real-life case study highlights some of the issues that surround the debate on freedom of information.

case study

Freedom of information campaign

Heather Brooke is a freedom of information campaigner who, within the space of a few years, has made a huge impact on British life. Her research has been a major factor in opening government to outside scrutiny.

Heather Brooke was educated in the United States of America (US), where she trained as a journalist. Working on newspapers in Washington and South Carolina she was well aware of how to use US freedom of information legislation. She came to Britain in 1997 to study literature but, in an unexpected twist, found herself again deploying her journalism skills.

She was living in a crime-ridden area and wanted to know what the local council was doing to combat it. 'The attitude of the Council was incredibly feudal. They wouldn't give me any information. Councils work for the public and the public should have access to their information.'

When the new UK Freedom of Information Act came into effect in 2005 many Members of Parliament (MPs) were surprised to find that it also applied to them. In 2007, some MPs proposed a parliamentary bill to exempt both Houses of Parliament from the provisions of the act, claiming it violated their privacy. There was a public outcry and the bill failed – but politicians were even less trusted than previously.

When Heather Brooke and other journalists started making freedom of information requests about staff, travel and housing expenses claimed by MPs, their requests were refused. The journalists appealed to the Information Commissioner – who after a year, ruled that some, but not all, information should be released. There was a further appeal by the media team and this time they won – all the information could be released.

However, the Speaker of the House of Commons appealed to the highest court (the Law Lords) not to release the information. He lost the appeal and it was agreed that the information would be released in October 2008. It wasn't! It was only in 2009 that the information finally became public because the *Daily Telegraph*, a leading newspaper, had paid a secret informant for the data.

The story, with its revelations of payments for second homes, gardens, entertainment and much more, dominated headlines for months. As a result, many MPs resigned or retired and six faced criminal charges.

The resulting publicity made Heather Brooke a media figure in her own right. A TV movie, *On Expenses*, dramatised her struggles. Her book and website helped ordinary citizens use freedom of information legislation. She says: '… we are seeing power shift back into the hands of people as they use the laws to ask searching questions about our public services.'

▼ Heather Brooke's book, *Your Right to Know* was designed as a guide to help people learn how to use the UK's Freedom of Information Act as well outline the difficulties they were likely to encounter.

v i e w p o i n t s

'The problem, however, is that requests under the Freedom of Information Act are becoming increasingly intrusive, particularly on issues such as the additional costs allowance. In that respect, they are getting into very personal realms – they are going behind the front door and into Members' homes... That is too intrusive and is going too far.'

Nick Harvey, MP, 7 February 2007

'It will be the height of hypocrisy if Parliament, having passed the Freedom of Information legislation, decided that we should be exempt from it.'

David Winnick, MP, 24 April 2007

CHAPTER 1

Freedom of information: an overview

The term 'freedom of information' can be interpreted in several ways. In its widest sense it means that, as a general principle, every person should have access to the information that they want or need in their lives. This may be to enable them to access personal information or to extend their education and learning. Even so, there are limitations on freedom of information. We wouldn't think it was right, for example, for people to have access to other people's private information, or to confidential medical records or to information that could be used for malicious or criminal purposes such as identity fraud.

Today, the term 'freedom of information' is mainly used in a more precise sense to refer to a citizen's right to access information from their government. Many countries now have freedom of information laws that state what rights a citizen has to government information and the responsibilities of government to fulfil these rights.

An accountable government

The principle behind such laws is that in a democratic society, a government should be accountable to the people whose votes put them in power and whose taxes

▼ What was the cost of combating the swine flu epidemic? A freedom of information request to the UK's Department of Health by the BBC was initially refused, but later allowed on appeal. It revealed that health authorities had spent £239 million on the swine flu vaccine up to April 2010. Many doses were unused and part of the order was later cancelled.

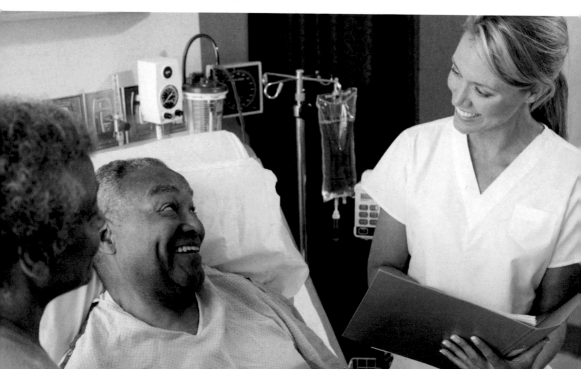

support the services provided by government. These services include things such as schools and hospitals, welfare services and policing. In a democratic society it is seen as right that citizens should be able to find out how services are organised, their cost and who uses them. Such information can help us to determine whether our taxes are being used well or badly and if the government is serving its citizens well or abusing its power.

In general, freedom of information laws refer only to government information. However, today many public services are run by private companies on behalf of governments, and governments own or part-own commercial companies, such as banks and transport facilities. In some cases freedom of information laws also apply to these bodies.

It's a fact

Today more information of all sorts is available than at any other time in history. Traditionally information was so valuable it was closely guarded and available only in libraries or to select groups of people. Today information is much more easily available, in multiple versions and disseminated through electronic technology, via websites and email. There is also more government information because government plays a bigger role in our lives, for example through tax collection and social security systems.

▼ A census is a nationwide attempt to count the entire population. The US census, held every ten years, asks a range of questions but individual details are kept confidential.

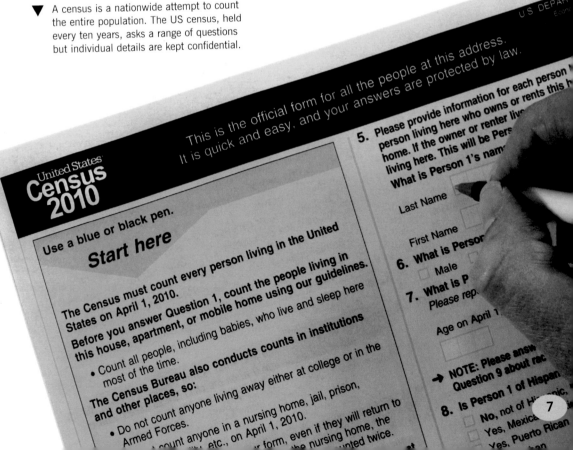

History of freedom of information

Today many people think of freedom of information as one of the basic rights of citizenship. However, the history of freedom of information is a fairly recent one, linked to the rise of more democratic and accountable governments. The Declaration of the Rights of Man and Citizens, drafted by the newly formed National Assembly during the French Revolution in 1789, stated that all citizens should have the right of access to government and public statements but did not state how this right could be put into effect.

The Universal Declaration of Human Rights of 1948, the founding document of the United Nations, links freedom of information to freedom of expression. Article 19 states: 'Everyone has the right to freedom of opinion and expression; this right includes freedom to hold opinions without interference and to seek, receive and impart information and ideas through any media and regardless of frontiers.' But Article 19 has nothing to say about the right of citizens to demand and receive information from their government.

Therefore it is surprising to learn that a law on freedom of information was first introduced almost 250 years ago. In 1766, the government of Sweden passed a law that allowed members of the public the right to obtain access to documents belonging to any area of government, local or national. This law was known as *Offentlighetsprincipen*, usually translated as 'Principle of Publicity'.

Why did Sweden lead the way?

Unlike most countries at the time, Sweden had some elements of a democratic society. There was a king with limited powers, a parliament with competing political parties and literate and socially aware citizens. The impetus for the 'Principle of Publicity' was to enable a new government to gain access to documents produced by a previous government and help stamp out secrecy and corruption.

▼ The Universal Declaration of Human Rights, signed by 48 countries, upholds the right to freedom of expression not the right to freedom of information.

THE UNIVERSAL DECLARATION OF **Human Rights**

UNITED NATIONS

However, the law later took on a wider purpose – to demonstrate that government was able to treat people equally, fairly and lawfully, and where this wasn't happening, enable people to lobby for changes in government.

Yet, for the following two centuries, no other country followed the Swedish example. It was only in the 1950s that Finland adopted freedom of information laws. But the real breakthrough came in 1966, when the US government enacted its first Freedom of Information Act.

It's a fact

The US Freedom of Information Act was passed thanks to the persistent efforts of Representative John Moss, a Democrat Congressman of California, who worked for eleven years to get the bill through Congress. President Lyndon B. Johnson was opposed to the bill and although he signed it into law in 1966, he did so without a public signing ceremony.

▼ On his first full day in office on 21 January 2009, President Obama signs an updated Freedom of Information Act (FOIA) to ensure that it works well for the twenty-first century. The FOIA, first passed in 1966, was previously updated in 1974 and 1996.

The spread of laws

The First US Freedom of Information Act (also known as FOIA) came about after years of lobbying by the media. The media was deeply frustrated by their failure to obtain the information they needed if they were to report on government activities accurately. A few years after the passing of FOIA in 1966 came the Watergate scandal. Diligent investigation by reporters Carl Bernstein and Bob Woodward of the *Washington Post* discovered that a break-in at the Democratic Party National Committee in Washington's Watergate Buildings was directly linked to a campaign to re-elect Republican President Nixon. They uncovered corruption and criminal activity that went all the way to the President's office, leading ultimately to the resignation of President Nixon.

Uncovering the Watergate scandal showed the importance of FOIA but also its limitations and, in 1974, the law was amended to place stronger responsibilities on government for greater openness in supplying information. In 1996 FOIA was again amended to include the new forms of electronic information such as email.

The US legislation proved to be highly influential and became a model for the rest of the world. Many countries enacted their own freedom of information laws (see timeline on page 47). In general, these were countries with democratically elected governments, a diverse media and active citizens' groups. In some countries it was the media who led the way, in others it was civil liberties groups and campaigning organisations.

▼ President Nixon resigns on 8 August 1974. Media coverage of the Watergate scandal had exposed his wrongdoings in such detail that he was forced from office.

case study

Stasi, the secret police

In the former German Democratic Republic, commonly known as East Germany, the secret police, the Stasi, kept detailed files on millions of people. The Stasi had spies everywhere – many were just ordinary people who were forced to spy on their family, friends and neighbours, under threat of punishment. Stasi files contained a huge amount of information, often inaccurate or biased, not just about the person being spied on, but the spies themselves.

▲ Some of the thousands of files collected by the Stasi secret police on their own citizens. Much of the information was collected by people spying on their neighbours.

In 1989, the East German government was overthrown in a peaceful revolution. Even as the old government disappeared, the Stasi started to destroy some of the most incriminating files. The authorities faced huge public anger and, since then, many files have been preserved and opened for inspection. The results have often been shattering as individuals discovered that they had been spied on by friends or family members, and that incidents years in the past had been used to deny them jobs or education. However, for many Germans, opening the Stasi files demonstrated the importance of freedom of information, both for government transparency and to support individual liberties. Even so, it was not until 2005 that a united Germany passed its first freedom of information law.

More acts to follow

More and more countries have adopted some form of freedom of information legislation. Many had suffered under past repressive governments, which not only denied them freedom to express their own opinions but also kept secret files on individual citizens. Often people demanded that their governments open the archives so that they could read what the state had recorded about their lives.

summary

▶ 'Freedom of information' means a citizen's right to access information from their government.

▶ The first country to grant a right to freedom of information was Sweden in 1766.

▶ The US government passed its first Freedom of Information Act in 1966.

CHAPTER 2

Freedom of information legislation

Given the large number of countries with freedom of information laws, it is not surprising that there are many variations in the ways such laws are framed and how they are used. Nevertheless there are some common features.

Similarities and differences

Overwhelmingly, freedom of information laws refer to government (public) information only, rather than private or individual information. However, what is defined as 'public' varies greatly. Organisations subject to freedom of information laws include central government, state or regional governments and local organisations, such as municipal councils or schools.

Because modern government is so large and complex, freedom of information may extend to thousands of organisations. For example, in the UK over 100,000 organisations are covered. In the US, with separate laws covering the federal government, states and territories, the list runs into millions. Sometimes areas of government activity are excluded from freedom of information requests – this is especially true of the military and security services in some countries, as often these are seen to need secrecy.

Most governments will establish a special agency, often called the Office of the Information Commissioner or something similar, to oversee freedom of information issues and ensure that the law works efficiently and in an unbiased way (for example, that it doesn't favour one political party or group over another). The law will state a time period for the request to be answered and the agency can intervene if requests are refused or delayed or if the response is incomplete. Sometimes the agency may also deal with appeals if a request is rejected although this aspect may be dealt with by a separate agency or through the court system.

◀ The Headquarters of the Central Intelligence Agency (CIA) in Langley, Virginia. The CIA is subject to US freedom of information legislation but often delays or refuses to release information requested (see page 35).

Who makes the requests?

Freedom of information requests can be made by individuals, or by organisations, such as political parties, campaigning groups or the media. In most countries, freedom of information requests are free of charge but some services charge fees for different types of information or for certain organisations (although individuals are rarely charged fees). In some countries, requests can be rejected if the information is easily available elsewhere or if they are considered frivolous, deliberately annoying or too costly.

Many types of information can be requested under freedom of information legislation. These range from laws, regulations and policy decisions to dates and events, statistics and accounts and much more. As a rule, requests will have some practical value – for example, revealing whether important decisions are being recorded, which organisations are lobbying government officials, how a service is being used and whether it is value for money.

It's a fact

The areas covered by freedom of information legislation normally include: defence (including military and intelligence); education (schools, colleges, universities); environmental issues (such as air quality and pollution issues); health (including hospitals and public health); the justice system (courts, jails, probation services); policing and security (including border controls); public housing; public transport; taxation; the welfare system (including benefit payments). Freedom of information also covers those who govern us, whether elected representatives (Congressmen, Members of Parliament etc) or appointed officials, paid and unpaid.

▼ In 2010, freedom of information requests were sent to every local authority in England, asking about school absences. The results were startling. Almost 12,000 students under 16 years-of-age were recorded as missing from school for a month or more at a time and around 1,200 seemed to have dropped out of school altogether.

Freedom of information and individual privacy

The right to freedom of information does not mean that everyone has a right to information about all aspects of other people's lives. What happens when a request for public information clashes with the rights of individuals, especially their right to privacy? The answer varies from country to country. In Sweden, individual tax returns are publicly available, whereas in most countries this would be considered a matter between the individual and the tax authorities. On the other hand, in all countries an individual's medical records are considered confidential between the doctor and the patient.

Critics of freedom of information say that requests for information might expose unnecessary details about individuals, for example, the names of employees or civil servants. Therefore some information records are returned with names omitted (often crudely blocked out). Supporters of freedom of information say that this practice is heavy-handed and is often used as a way to absolve officials of responsibility for their poor decision-making or bad practice, and that, in any case, a person in a public position such as a manager or high-ranking civil servant, should not hide behind a wall of privacy.

Critics defend this saying that blame for errors should not be heaped on the shoulders of civil servants, who are just carrying out their jobs. But supporters would say that civil servants are acting on behalf of the public, not as private individuals. In any case, much of the information provided under freedom of information is about facts and figures, not personal details.

case study

Public employees in Illinois

How do you balance individual privacy with freedom of information? In 2009 the state of Illinois decided to update its Freedom of Information Act. The new law stated: 'The disclosure of information that bears on the public duties of public employees and officials shall not be considered an invasion of personal privacy.' In other words, government must respond to requests for information about the work of public servants. This includes individual 'performance evaluations' (how individual staff are judged to be doing their jobs, their grades and salaries).

This proved highly controversial. Some groups, including teachers and law enforcement staff, were exempted from the provision and there have been moves to exempt all public employees. Trade unions protested that disclosing job evaluations would be an invasion of personal privacy. Evaluation results might not be interpreted correctly and as a result a worker might be penalised or subject to public condemnation. Supporters of freedom of information say that including job evaluations enables the public to know that individual employees are qualified and capable of doing their jobs, and that making some groups exempt undermines public trust in government.

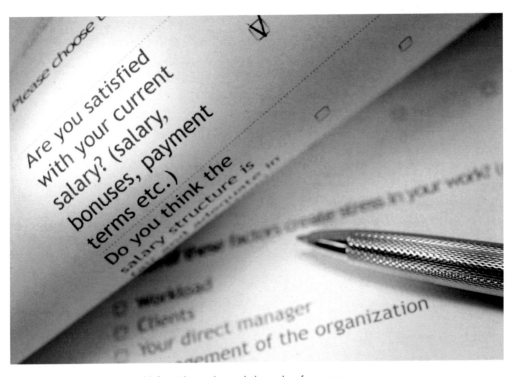

▲ In some countries personal information such as salaries and performance evaluations are subject to freedom of information laws. However, some people argue that this infringes upon people's privacy and, as such, is ethically unacceptable.

viewpoints

'While it is possible to identify and publish information on how much benefit people receive, there is next to no public knowledge of how much tax people pay... To redress the balance, contributions to the exchequer should be made subject – as in Sweden – to freedom of information legislation.'

Michael Egan, letter to the *Guardian*, 8 October 2010

'The difficulty lies with our responsibility to put in place a process to make sure that we don't breach someone's human rights... If someone asks how much John Smith in planning gets paid, we could put the question on the website but what we can't do is tell them the answer because it would breach his rights.'

Councillor Ian Greenwood, Bradford Council, as reported in the *Telegraph & Argus*, 4 October 2010

summary

▶ A wide range of organisations is covered by freedom of information laws.

▶ There are many different types of information that people can request.

▶ Freedom of information issues are usually overseen by an independent agency that can make judgements and hear appeals.

▶ There may be a conflict between a right to freedom of information and an individual's right to privacy.

CHAPTER 3

Freedom of information and government

One of the driving ideas behind freedom of information is that it makes a government more accountable to citizens. After all, people vote the government into power and the government then provides services from the taxes paid by individuals and companies. Surely those electors and taxpayers should have the right to know what the government is doing in their name and with their money?

A pillar of society?

Supporters of freedom of information legislation see it as one of the pillars of a democratic society, along with other human rights such as the right to vote, freedom of expression and freedom of the press. They say that freedom of information makes it possible for citizens to see what their government does in their name, in other words to make government open and accountable – this is often described as 'transparency'. Without such legislation government will remain closed and unaccountable, making decisions in secret, without consultation and without informing the public.

Why is government decision-making closed and secretive? Some people say that it is just the natural way government – or indeed any large organisation – operates.

▼ Government ministers, led by US President Barack Obama (front row, third from left), after at a Cabinet meeting. Should details of Cabinet meetings be made available to the public?

Or a culture of secrecy?

Other people feel that it is government itself that is at fault because it has developed a 'culture of secrecy', which is passed on from one generation to another. Therefore freedom of information provides one of the essential 'checks and balances' which balances the power of government against the power of law and opens up the workings of government to citizens.

On the other hand, critics of freedom of information say that it simply isn't possible to have every piece of government information made accessible to the public. Sometimes decisions must be made quickly and decisively, without extensive consultation. If every single meeting and decision has to be recorded in minute detail, not only does it take up extra time and resources, but it also places decision-makers under constant suspicion. Who will speak out frankly if every thought is to be recorded on file? Who will be willing to engage in 'thinking the unthinkable' (looking at all the choices) if a memo immediately becomes common knowledge? Surely what will happen is that decision-makers will find ways around the restrictions, meeting in private or communicating informally, without notes, or even destroying records.

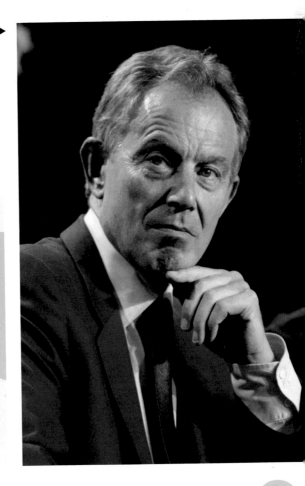

Tony Blair was British Prime Minister for ten years, from 1997 to 2007. His government introduced the UK's first Freedom of Information Act in 2000. However, despite his early enthusiasm, he later came to regret the law, saying it was impractical for good government. However, his critics said that it was because it revealed aspects of government which he wanted to remain secret.

viewpoints

'Our commitment to a Freedom of Information Act is clear, and I reaffirm it here tonight. We want to end the obsessive and unnecessary secrecy which surrounds government activity and make government Information available to the public unless there are good reasons not to do so.'
Tony Blair, leader of the opposition Labour Party, 25 March 1996

'The worst thing I ever did in government was to introduce the Freedom of information Act... It is not practical for good government.'
Tony Blair, former Prime Minister, 2010

The costs involved

Critics often focus on the costs that freedom of information places on government, both in financial and staff terms. While it is easy to talk about the benefits of freedom of information, in reality it poses real problems for those who have to deliver it. The government has to draft and adopt a new law, agree how it has to be implemented and establish an organisation to oversee the law. It has to publicise the new law in government departments and train civil servants to teach them how use it. The government must also ensure that the public knows and understands how the law will operate.

However, critics say, the real costs come when the law is in operation. Hard-working civil servants are diverted from carrying out essential tasks because they are flooded with numerous freedom of information requests, some of them ignorant, frivolous or ridiculous. Many requests involve collecting statistics of little value or use outside the interest of the enquirer. Enquirers may return again and again with similar requests. Some requests involve asking for copies of documents from years before, when standards of collection and indexing were very different and have little or no relevance to current government practices. In many departments, extra staff are employed just to reply to freedom of information requests.

Are these costs exaggerated?

Supporters say the costs are greatly exaggerated. While freedom of information legislation does create new tasks for government, most of the costs are at the beginning of the process, mainly in the creation of a new organisation to oversee the laws and initial training. However, this process happens with many new laws – it is a normal part of government. Similarly, civil servants regularly collect statistics, and write and retrieve documents. A freedom of information law will mean that these functions will improve and that such information is likely to be placed in a government publication or website, rather than hidden from the public.

Supporters say that once the law is in operation, then requests should be dealt with smoothly and efficiently. If this doesn't happen, it is because government departments are obstructive and unwilling to co-operate. In other words, it is the culture of secrecy that is the problem, not the cost of freedom of information. In any case, supporters believe that the real value of freedom of information cannot be measured in money but in the trust it creates between citizens and the government.

◄ The costs involved in researching and supplying information under freedom of information requests can be expensive. Some people argue that meeting these costs is not a fair use of public money

case study

Freedom of information campaign

BC Ferries operates a vital public transport link along Canada's west coast. Originally BC Ferries was a government-owned company and so had to answer queries under British Colombia's Freedom of Information Act. When BC Ferries was sold to private owners in 2003, it became exempt from freedom of information provisions.

Many people were unhappy with the situation, arguing that although the company was privately owned it still provided an essential public service. They had many questions.

How were fare prices set? How were routes and timetables decided? How many accidents and near-accidents had been recorded? Why had payments to managers increased, especially in light of widespread public dissatisfaction with services? Persistent lobbying by media and consumer groups finally paid off and the law was changed to make BC Ferries subject to freedom of information legislation.

In October 2010, BC Ferries began responding to freedom of information requests, although it charged fees for these requests, and placing answers on its website.

▼ When BC Ferries went from government to private ownership, the company was no longer subject to freedom of information legislation. However, public dissatisfaction and a lively media campaign was able to reverse the decision.

Putting your trust in government

Many people say that they have little trust in their government. They are suspicious both of elected politicians and government officials. How often have you heard someone declaring that all politicians are devious and corrupt and that public servants are lazy and overpaid?

Some critics, including politicians, say that freedom of information laws, combined with media attention, has increased criticism and undermined trust in government. Media attention given to formerly hidden information gives the impression that government is wasteful or extravagant. Highlighting the corruption or hypocrisy of a few politicians lowers public esteem for democratic institutions and discourages hardworking honest people from taking up a political career. Meanwhile private sector organisations are allowed to commit the same errors or crimes free from public scrutiny.

Nowhere to hide

However, supporters of freedom of information say that it is an important tool in democratic government. If people distrust politicians and officials then it is up to them to raise standards in public life. Openness can reveal where government gets things right and where mistakes are made. Rather than undermining trust, freedom of information will create trust because people know that government cannot hide behind a wall of secrecy.

▼ The House of Commons, the lower house of the UK Parliament, in session. In July 2015, the government announced that it would establish a five-person commission to review the working of the Freedom of Information Act. There are fears that it would tighten access and increase costs for those using the act.

case study

WikiLeaks – information goes global

As the Internet extends information beyond country borders, independent websites have developed to display government information not normally available to the public.

WikiLeaks is the most famous of these websites. It aims 'to bring important news and information to the public' by accepting, checking and publishing information from whistle-blowers anywhere in the world. Since 2007, it has used cutting edge technology to publish documents online in many languages. In 2010 WikiLeaks obtained hundreds of thousands of US documents and images (including videos) on military involvement in Iraq and Afghanistan and confidential diplomatic communications. The contents made headlines across the world.

Supporters claim that WikiLeaks has revealed information on government policies, activities and behaviour that are unethical, hypocritical and embarrassing. They say disclosure will force government to be more open and transparent in their activities and will help root out corrupt and criminal behaviour. *Time* magazine said that the WikiLeaks model 'could become as important a journalistic tool as the Freedom of Information Act.'

Critics say that WikiLeaks itself is unethical because it reveals information which is secret for good reason – for example, because it is confidential advice to government or vital to national security. Rather than supporting freedom of information it will undermine it, putting people's lives at risk.

▼ The WikiLeaks website reveals one of the many thousands of classified documents on US military encounters in Afghanistan. The documents were passed secretly to WikiLeaks by a whistle-blower.

Does freedom of information reduce corruption?

One of the reasons behind early freedom of information legislation was that it would expose corruption in government. Corruption can take many forms. It often involves secretly passing money to government officials for special treatment. This might range from something as simple as an individual paying a policeman not to issue a speeding ticket, or as complex as a giant company funnelling money to officials through a network of 'shell' (fake) companies in order to gain a government contract. In other cases government ministers or officials may give favourable treatment to individuals or powerful groups, knowing that they will be rewarded in the future.

Some people defend corruption, usually on the practical grounds that it helps to 'get things done'. The most common argument is that in some countries corruption and bribery are normal business practice and those who don't take part will lose out. However, most people believe that corruption is deeply unfair. It adds extra hidden costs to businesses, which are paid by consumers and society as a whole. Corruption favours the rich, who can pay, over the poor, who cannot, and enriches dishonest people over those who follow the rules. A corrupt government is distrusted and sometimes hated by its people.

Does freedom of information legislation make governments less corrupt? In theory, it should. Making government information and practices open to public scrutiny should give everyone equal access to important information about procedures, jobs and contracts. For example, a person

It's a fact

Journalists from the *Sydney Morning Herald* used the Australian Freedom of Information Act to reveal close ties between Ministry of Defence officials and arms companies. In a three-year period between 2007 and 2010, arms companies provided more than 110 free dinners, lunches, theatre and football tickets to top defence officials. The Ministry of Defence said that any contact perceived as improper 'would be investigated and appropriate action undertaken'.

A sign in 2009 reads that this government building in Nairobi, Kenya is a corruption free zone. However, how can Kenya's citizens be sure the government is not corrupt? Could freedom of information reassure people?

▲ Paying money 'under the counter' to obtain favourable treatment is common in many countries. Freedom of information can play a role in exposing corruption.

faced with what they believe to be an unfair speeding fine would know the procedure for appealing the police decision, rather than trying to bribe the officer. Every company that wants to bid for a government contract would know the exact procedures to follow and all information would be publicly available so they could not make secret bids or falsify figures.

But does this always happen in practice?

Even supporters of freedom of information recognise that an open government cannot always prevent corruption. It also needs good practice throughout government, respect for the rule of law and a willingness to find and punish wrongdoers.

However, freedom of information legislation can play a role in helping to expose and deal with corruption – if the right questions are asked. For example, a freedom of information request might reveal the numbers of police officers found taking bribes from motorists, and whether and how they were punished.

On the other hand, it is much harder to unravel a complex and sophisticated fraud as few people would begin to know what questions to ask and to understand the answers.

summary

▶ Supporters of freedom of information claim that it makes government more open, accountable and effective and less secretive.

▶ Critics say that freedom of information places a heavy and costly burden on government and can undermine people's trust in government.

▶ Freedom of information, together with strong laws, can help to expose government corruption.

CHAPTER 4

Who uses freedom of information?

Supporters of freedom of information laws frequently describe them as tools that will open up the everyday workings of government to ordinary citizens. But how does freedom of information work in practice?

Where freedom of information laws exist, individuals do use them. Many are seeking their own personal records (such as social security or tax details or medical records). Although the situation varies from country to country, most freedom of information requests come not from individuals but from companies, the media and special interest campaigners. Some politicians also use freedom of information legislation, as a basis for asking questions, campaigning and developing policy.

▼ Public Service Minister David Clark holds up a copy of the UK government's proposals for a new Freedom of Information law on 11 December 1997. The law was passed in 2000 and came into effect in 2005.

The number of freedom of information requests to US government agencies continues to increase year by year. The Office for Information Policy reported that in 2014 there were 714,231 requests to federal agencies compared to 557,825 in 2009 – an increase of almost 30%. By far the highest number of requests, 291,241, comprising 26% of the total, were to the Department of Homeland Security. The report stated that 91% of the total requests were answered in full or in part but there were still large backlogs of unanswered requests – almost 160,000 in 2014.

Getting the information

Whatever the law might say, it can be difficult to access government information. You need to have a clear idea of what information you need and which part of government it comes from – something that is not always obvious. You have to check that the information isn't already available; perhaps in a government publication or on a website. You need to write and deliver your request to the right official in the correct department. In a well-functioning system these details should be easily available on a website and the request and answers delivered through email, but this isn't always the case.

Answers should be delivered within a specified timeframe but many are not. Other requests are refused or not answered at all. Delays can continue for months – sometimes even years. When an answer arrives it may be incomplete or unsatisfactory. It may be written in bureaucratic language or technical jargon, which may be hard for a non-expert to understand. And, at times the documentation supplied is so extensive that substantial charges are levied. All this means that following up freedom of information requests often takes skill and persistence.

Anyone should be able to make a freedom of information request by following some simple steps. Firstly, decide what information you want to obtain. Remember, it should have some public interest or use. The next step is to find out what department or agency holds the information. It is important to check carefully to see if it is already available in publications or on their website. When sending in your request, word it clearly, precisely and politely. You can usually apply by email as well as by post. Ensure that you keep a careful record of your request and the deadline for an answer. If the answer is late or incomplete, go back and repeat your request. Once you have the information, think of the best way to use it.

The US is by far the country with the highest total of freedom of information requests, both by number – one and a half million requests each year – and compared to population size, with 492 requests for each 100,000 inhabitants (see table page 28).

The media

One of the main consumers of information is the media. This is a vast group ranging from multi-national media empires to a local paper or even an individual blogger. It includes press (newspapers and magazines), broadcast (radio and television) and electronic media (websites, blogs and social networking). Freedom of information is especially suited to newspapers and news websites. A freedom of information request may lead to an interesting and unique news story, sometimes even to a change in government policy.

The media is normally in a better position to pursue freedom of information requests than individuals as they have more funds and can call on legal advice if a request is not forthcoming. It is worth remembering that the US freedom of information legislation, which has been used as a model in many other countries, came about precisely because the media was continually frustrated when trying to get information from government.

Some critics claim that freedom of information laws make it too easy for the media to gain information, rather than use traditional investigative journalism. But supporters point out that today a freedom of information request is a normal tool of journalism, taught during journalist training. Without freedom of information legislation, the media might resort to underhand or illegal ways of getting information, for example, paying informants, entrapment or illegal wiretapping or hacking into a private phone.

Good or bad?

But does the media use freedom of information carefully and responsibly? Many people would say the answer is no – that this is not always the case. Rather, the media pursues requests that make for a good story, preferably one involving money, sex or scandal, rather than the more mundane issues that deeply affect people's lives. Critics say that rather than supporting open government, the media launches vendettas, for example

It's a fact

When Prince Harry, a member of the Royal family, undertook military service in Afghanistan the UK media agreed not to report it, fearing it would endanger British troops. However, in February 2008, when reports appeared in non-UK media, the secret was out and Prince Harry was hastily withdrawn from Afghanistan.

Prince Harry was withdrawn from Afghanistan ▶ after information was leaked to the media about his deployment. Some people argue this is an example of freedom of information being abused and endangering lives.

In many parts of the world the media is not able to report news stories freely, especially those critical of the government. They face censorship or closure if they displease the government. This paper in Bahrain, *Akhbar Al-Khaleej*, was ordered to suspend publication in June 2009 after publishing an article on elections in Iran.

against a particular government department or politician, and follows up causes that reflect their support for a particular policy or political party. Some media requests can be invasions of an individual's privacy, rather than a genuine information request, for example looking for details of a person's marriage or family life.

Even supporters of freedom of information would admit that not all the outcomes of freedom of information requests are useful or worthwhile. Nevertheless, they feel that overall, the media uses freedom of information laws in a responsible way. They say that it has helped to highlight otherwise hidden information, bring important issues to public attention and reform public life.

viewpoints

'The Freedom of Information Act is something this government is committed to but we want to make sure that it works well and fairly. It is on occasions misused by those who want to generate stories for the media. That isn't acceptable.'
Chris Graying, UK Attorney-General, speaking in Parliament, 29 October 2015

'Government is a closed shop. The Freedom of Information Act is one of the tools that should be used to open up government.'
Bob Woodward, journalist, *Yale Daily News*, US, 19 November 2010

It's a fact

It is not always easy to get to the truth behind government statistics given through freedom of information requests. Take hospital death rates after operations for example. The statistics may reveal hospitals with higher death rates than others. Is this because the operating teams are less talented or experienced or the facilities less modern or well-equipped? Perhaps – but it may be because the hospital accepts patients who are very old or very young or have more complex conditions. A hospital serving a poor neighbourhood is also likely to have higher death rates than one in a wealthier area. Many other factors may need to be taken into account to discover which hospitals are performing the best.

How campaigners use freedom of information

Today increasing numbers of campaigners, both organisations and individuals, use freedom of information laws to get access to government information. This sort of activity can range from something as simple as a neighbourhood group seeking plans on road widening or crime statistics in their locality, to a national organisation looking for statistics on issues as varied as immigrant numbers, breaches of clean air laws or prison conditions. Once they have the information, they can publicise it through their members or the media, and use it to place pressure on politicians and government officials, for example by lobbying, mass emails, meetings or demonstrations.

Most campaigners are open about their motives and seek specific information that will aid their cause. Some critics argue that this is not always a legitimate use of freedom of information. They point out that large, well-resourced organisations, or educated and committed individuals, are in a much better position to pursue information requests and publish the outcomes, than small groups and poor communities. Supporters admit that this may well be true but it is a problem of an unequal society, rather than freedom of information itself. They believe that the way to narrow such gaps is to use simple language, have good information on procedures and helpful officials.

A valuable tool?

Critics also say that campaigners only use information that they find useful and ignore, or even distort, material that isn't helpful. So two opposing groups can draw different conclusions from much the same information. Supporters feel very differently. For them freedom of information is a valuable tool which enables citizens and not-for-profit organisations to challenge powerful government through a combination of accurate information and public opinion.

This table shows the number of freedom of information requests made in 2009 by different countries.

Country	Number of requests per year	Total number of requests per 100,000 inhabitants
United States of America	1,500,000	492
Bulgaria	14,000	175
Mexico	105,000	98
Japan	100,000	80
Ireland	3,000	75
Romania	15,000	68
Croatia	3,000	67
United Kingdom (excl. Scotland)	85,000	64
Scotland	3,000	60
Turkey	39,000	56
Israel	3,000	46
South Africa	20,000	45
Australia	4,000	20
Finland	500	10
Netherlands	1,200	7

Source: Roger Vleugels, Overview of all 90 FOIAs, 7 September 2009

case study

Government electronic spying

What does your government really know about you? Most people feel that the government has no business in intruding into your private life, and that the messages you send and receive should also be private as long as they are within the law.

So many Americans were deeply shocked when a young man called Edward Snowden revealed that US intelligence agencies were regularly collecting information on the electronic communications - phone calls, texts, emails and instant messaging - of millions of Americans as well as of foreign citizens, including world leaders. The agencies believed that this helped to detect and prevent terrorist actions.

Snowden was deeply perturbed and believed that this was wrong and unconstitutional. He claimed that he reported his concerns to his managers but was ignored. In 2013 he decided that he had no choice but to release the information, including millions of intelligence files, to the world media to bring attention to the issue.

Today Edward Snowden lives in exile in Russia. He has been told that he will be arrested as a spy if he returns to the USA. Some people regard him as a hero, others as a traitor.

◀ Politicians and the media play a prominent role in exposing government secrecy. Here US Senators Dianne Feinstein and Ron Wyden participate in a news conference on the Senate Select Committee on Iraq. A report said that the reasons for the US going to war in Iraq were based on inaccurate intelligence reports and poor judgements.

summary

▶ Freedom of information laws are used by a wide range of people and organisations for many different purposes.

▶ In the US companies are the largest users of freedom of information legislation.

▶ The media and campaigners increasingly use freedom of information laws.

CHAPTER 5

Off limits – who decides what is secret?

Should all government business be open to public scrutiny? Governments believe there should be limits on public access to some types of material – and many people agree. However, there is continuing disagreement over what these restrictions, known as 'exemptions', should be.

The need for secrets

The problem is that there is no agreement about where you draw the line between 'dangerous' information and 'safe' information. In some countries few documents are classified (kept secret), in others a great many. But even when the law says that information should be available, government officials may refuse access on the grounds that it would threaten national security.

Most freedom of information systems have some limits on disclosure. One method is supplying material in a censored or 'redacted' format. This is where a document is made available but with some text removed (often literally with a black marker pen). In the most straightforward cases, this may be just removing the names of junior officials or office staff, usually for privacy reasons. But in other cases large amounts of text is removed so that documents are almost unreadable and the information value is minimal.

Other documents are classed as 'historical' and placed in archives where they remain hidden from public examination until it is deemed safe for them to be opened. This is usually after the politicians and officials

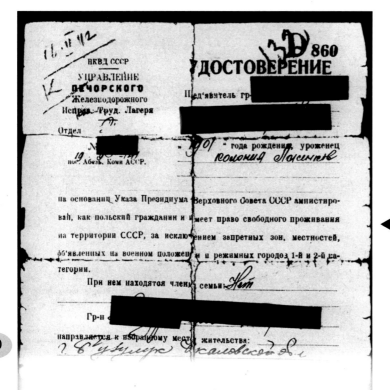

◀ A document in Russia from archives of the former Soviet Union is heavily redacted with thick black lines through 'sensitive' information.

▲ Historical archives in Barcelona, Spain. The documents were seized by the
victorious fascist forces during the civil war of 1936–39 and were only
returned to the Catalonia National Archives in 2006.

involved have died or retired and the
information can no longer endanger the
public or embarrass the government.
Supporters of freedom of information feel
that the time limits are too long, especially
for information which is not sensitive and
which may already be well known.

Official Secrets Act

However, in many countries, the biggest
barriers are laws on secrecy. This may be
one law, usually called the 'Official Secrets
Act' or something similar, or a series of
laws, often obscure and little known.
These laws cover areas deemed secret
and list penalties for breaking the law.
A government may have one law
supporting freedom of information and
another keeping information secret. Some
countries have attempted to deal with this
situation. For example, when New Zealand
passed its first freedom of information law

in 1982, it also abolished its Official
Secrets Act, and put any exemptions
into the new law.

It's a fact

In the UK most historical documents
are classified under the '30-year rule'.
These documents include notes of meetings
of the Prime Minister and Cabinet. Usually
when documents are released after
30 years, they receive considerable
publicity, as they cast a new light on the
problems and pressures of government.
Such material is of great interest to
researchers and historians. In 2010 the
government announced that the time limit
would be reduced to 20 years. In Scotland,
the limit is 15 years.

Staying safe and secure

Areas classified as 'national security' are highly controversial. They usually include the military (at home or overseas), police and the intelligence services (often called espionage and popularly known as spies), as well as individuals or companies who do business with these organisations. In some countries these areas are completely closed to scrutiny, in others they are partly open and in others there is a great deal of public access.

For example in the US, the Pentagon (the Department of Defense), the Federal Bureau of Investigation (FBI) and other police forces at federal and state level and the Central Intelligence Agency (CIA) are all subject to freedom of information laws. However, in practice, these agencies have often been reluctant to disclose information, sometimes delaying requests for years (see fact panel page 35). In addition, they can be called on to give evidence in public before Congressional committees. Over the years, this has revealed a large amount of information to public view. Transparency is also aided by the fact that the US does not have an Official Secrets Act. In contrast, in the UK, while the Ministry of Defence and police forces are covered by freedom of information legislation, the intelligence services are exempt, although they may be called upon to give evidence to parliamentary committees.

There are other areas where government secrecy covers actions that are dangerous, murky or corrupt. One example is the relationship between government and arms companies who manufacture hugely expensive and dangerous weapons, either for their own government or for export. Governments and companies are often very close, where contracts for weapons run into billions of dollars, yet dealings which may be illegal or unethical are hidden from public view. This is sometimes on security grounds, but also because disclosure might damage international relations or break commercial confidentiality.

▼ The Pentagon in Washington DC, home of the US Department of Defence. Within its walls are many miles of valuable documents, some deemed to be highly sensitive and secret.

case study

Uncovering arms deals

Campaign Against Arms Trade (CAAT) is a long-established UK group that regularly uses freedom of information legislation to expose the truths behind international arms deals. A major aim has been to reveal the story behind the UK's largest ever arms deal, worth over £40 billion. Under the deal, known as *Al Yamamah* ('The Dove'), in the 1980s British Aerospace (now called BAE Systems) sold Saudi Arabia hundreds of Tornado and Hawk jets.

However, from the beginning, *Al Yamamah* has been surrounded by secrecy and there have been regular allegations of corruption in the form of huge 'commissions' (illegal payments) to those involved in negotiating the deal. CAAT has attempted to find documents on *Al Yamamah* but found that information requests have been refused or documents supplied in redacted formats. On one occasion, documents already placed in the National Archives (and therefore available to the public) were hastily removed by the Ministry of Defence. However, CAAT had copied the documents and published them on its website.

Under the 30-year rule (see page 31), some of the documents relating to the Al Yamamah arms deal have been made public. They shed new light on the government's role in securing the deal, including stressing the secrecy surrounding it. However, many documents are heavily redacted (censored) and the full extent of the "commissions" on the deal remains a secret, kept under lock and key.

▼ Supporters of Campaign Against Arms Trade demonstrate against a backdrop of weapons on display at Farnborough Air Show, UK.

National security or legitimate interest?

Is the concept of 'national security' a valid one? People feel that it is often used as an excuse to suppress knowledge of areas of public life that government does not want citizens to know about.

Supporters of freedom of information are often frustrated by the restrictions of 'national security'. They may be so strictly drawn that it is impossible to penetrate them, or conversely, so vaguely worded so that they cover almost any area of government activity. The right to appeal against the restrictions may also be limited or ineffectual. Secrecy may affect civil liberties if an individual cannot access their personal files and has no idea of the information the government holds on them – information that may be unfair or inaccurate.

But defenders of the restrictions believe that these are reasonable and proportionate and enable important government agencies to operate in ways that, by their nature, have to be secret, for example, protecting soldiers in a war zone, or tracking criminals, extremists or terrorists. They say that revealing information will put military and security services at risk and can endanger society as a whole, by putting information in the wrong hands.

A wider debate

The larger debate is not just about freedom of information but about what makes a society safer and more secure. Increasingly many people believe that in a peaceful and democratic society, government should be open about all its work. They say that openness brings trust in government and encourages people to use peaceful and lawful ways to resolve problems and conflicts. But others say that even a democratic country faces threats, such as crime and terrorism, and that a government must be able to keep some information from public view in order to be able to keep society safe.

◀ A soldier in a war zone. Many governments argue freedom of information will endanger the lives of military and security forces.

It's a fact

In 1992 the National Security Archive, a research group in the US, filed a freedom of information request for a series of CIA documents known as the 'Family Jewels'. It was only 15 years later, in 2007, that the documents were released in a heavily censored format. Even so, the 702 pages of documents from the 1960s and 1970s revealed a huge array of wrongdoing. It showed that the CIA had spied on more than 300,000 American citizens, including students and journalists, although it was specifically barred from doing so. Other documents revealed illegal wiretaps, break-ins and assassination plots. Critics point out some of the information had already been revealed by the media and before Congress, and that much was still missing.

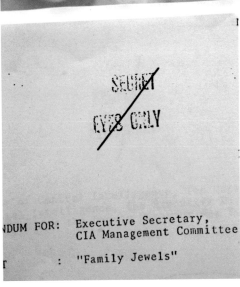

SECRET
EYES ONLY

NDUM FOR: Executive Secretary,
             CIA Management Committee

        :   "Family Jewels"

▲ For your eyes only. For many years CIA documents called the 'Family Jewels' were kept from freedom of information campaigners. The documents detailed many cases of wrongdoing by the government security agency.

viewpoints

'Information belongs to the American people, despite our government's insistence that it does not. In this age of terrorism, knee-jerk secrecy aims to protect us from the evils of the world. In practice, though it might just do the opposite.'
Tom Blanton, Director, National Security Archive, *USA Today*, 13 March 2007

'We live in a dirty and dangerous world. There are some things that the general public does not need to know, and shouldn't. I believe democracy flourishes when the government can take legitimate steps to keep its secrets and when the press can decide whether to print what it knows.'
Katharine Graham, former owner of the *Washington Post*, speaking at the CIA Headquarters, Langley, Virginia, 1988

summary

▶ Government information on military and security issues is often exempt from freedom of information laws or heavily censored.

▶ Many 'historical documents' are placed in archives and may not be opened for 20 or 30 years.

▶ Supporters of freedom of information say that 'national security' considerations are unnecessary and can be used to conceal wrongdoing. Critics say that restrictions are needed to protect national security.

CHAPTER 6

Blowing the whistle

Sometimes an individual feels so strongly about hidden information that he or she takes action to bring it to public attention, even if this means breaking the law. These people are known as 'whistle-blowers' because, like a football referee, they are prepared to blow the whistle when they spot wrongdoing.

Who are whistle-blowers?

A whistle-blower can be an employee, contractor, public servant, board member or a concerned individual. The organisation may be a government department, a public authority, a commercial company or a not-for-profit organisation. A whistle-blower may be concerned about one or more issues – fraud, corruption, criminal activity, falsifying facts or statistics, health and safety breaches or mistreatment of staff, patients or customers.

Most whistle-blowers first try to bring up their concerns with their organisation. However, this can be difficult. How can they talk with their manager if the manager is part of the problem? What happens if their concerns are dismissed or ignored? They may find that they are mistreated, threatened, demoted or dismissed from their jobs. They come to the conclusion that the only way forward is to speak to an outsider of their concerns. They may go to the police or a regulatory body (often referred to as a 'watchdog'). Other whistle-blowers talk to lawyers or the media – perhaps via the press, a radio or television programme. In doing so, some may face legal action by their employers.

It's a fact

The term 'whistle-blower' does not always translate easily. In other languages, they are given different names which serve the same meaning. For example, in Dutch, the term is *Klokkenluider* which translates as 'bell-ringer'.

Heroes or troublemakers?

Although the numbers of whistle-blowers are relatively small, their situation has captured the public imagination, becoming the subject of books and films.

case study

Uncovering financial fraud

Sherron Watkins worked in the finance department at Enron, one of the largest energy companies in the US. She became increasingly uneasy about the company's accounting practices whereby assets were inflated in value while losses were hidden in complex systems. Realising that Enron's accounting amounted to large-scale fraud, in 2001 she sent a detailed memo to the chief executive. He ignored her warning and later that year Enron filed for bankruptcy, amid financial scandal. The next year, Watkins's concerns were aired before a Congressional committee. Watkins says that she was not strictly a whistle-blower as she did not take her concerns outside the company.

'We need whistle-blowers. They keep our institutions honest. From Enron, to Walkerton, to the intelligence failures around 9/11, whistle-blowers have made a huge contribution to informing the public and fighting corruption and incompetence.'
Micheal Anderson, 'Don't shoot the Whistleblower', www.tyee.ca, Canada, 14 March 2005

'In the post-Enron era, these self-appointed do-gooders are granted breathless audiences by Congress, extolled on national television and lauded by *Time* magazine as Persons of the Year. But some whistle-blowers are motivated by greed, willing to stretch the truth for profit.'
Neil Weinberg, 'The Dark Side of Whistleblowing', www.forbes.com, 14 March 2005

Many people admire whistle-blowers, believing that they are heroes, dedicated to exposing the truth. Critics say that they are trouble-makers, discontented with their job and position, or attention-seekers.

A few would even go so far as to say that whistle-blowers are traitors, to their company, government or country.

In fact, in many countries whistle-blowers have some protection under the law. For example, in the US, a number of court cases have established that whistle-blowing is justified in some circumstances where the employer takes no action to stop the wrongdoing. In other court cases, juries have delivered 'not guilty' verdicts because they felt that the whistle-blower was acting in an ethical manner, even if he or she was breaking the law.

▼ In 2003 Katharine Gun was working as a translator at the UK's Government Communications Headquarters (known as GCHQ) when she received a US request for help to 'bug' (engage in illegal surveillance) the UN offices of six countries in the run-up to the Iraq war. Katharine Gun was horrified and became a whistle-blower, taking the information to the media. She was dismissed from her job and arrested under the Official Secrets Act. However, at the last minute the government dropped the charges against her.

The whistle-blower and his wife

India is a democratic country, but it is one where bribery is common. Mr M.N. Vijayakumar, a public servant in Karnataka state in southern India, repeatedly reported cases of corruption to the civil service and the state anti-corruption watchdog. At first he had some success but later his reports were ignored. As a result of his reporting on the wrongdoings, he was transferred from job to job, place to place, and his life and his family were threatened.

His wife J.N. Jayashree came up with a novel solution to protect her husband. In 2007 she started writing a blog, which went on to become a website, with details about her husband's work and his fight against corruption. Mrs Jayashree says, 'It is harder to kill a man who has a bit of Internet renown. We are building a fortress of people to protect him.' The website, called Fight Corruption NOW, has become well-known in India and receives information and enquiries from the public.

The website also contains details on how people can use India's Right to Information Act. Mrs Jayashree says that the act, which came into effect in 2005, is an important tool for Indians who want to see justice and an end to corruption. She is also campaigning or a law that will give legal protection to whistle-blowers.

▲ Mrs Jayashree working on her anti-corruption website, which also contains information on how to use India's Right to Information Act.

Do whistle-blowers aid freedom of information?

What is the connection between whistle-blowing and freedom of information? Many people would argue that there is a direct link because without strong freedom of information laws, whistle-blowing may be the only way to bring hidden issues to public view.

However, there are also problems with this view. Not all whistle-blowers are government employees – many come from private companies not covered by freedom of information legislation. Whistle-blowing also goes well beyond information issues into areas of behaviour and conduct that would not always be revealed by freedom of information requests. Unsurprisingly, materials documenting criminal or unethical behaviour are generally unavailable or have been destroyed, while other possible evidence, such as reports of meetings or telephone conversations,

are unreliable or hearsay (reported second hand). However, it may be possible to capture evidence through other means, such as wiretaps, covert filming and monitoring of emails.

Many people believe that whistle-blowers should be supported and protected. Within organisations employees should be able to speak of their concerns without being penalised. For example, some companies have an 'ethics monitor' or an 'ethics hotline' – a person or phone number where employees can speak to someone in confidence. Governments can also support whistle-blowers who reveal wrongdoing, although many do not. In some countries whistle-blowers face discrimination, public shaming, jail and death threats. Independent organisations, such as the National Whistle-blowers Center in the US, advise whistle-blowers and lobby for laws to protect them.

summary

► Whistle-blowers are people who are prepared to expose wrongdoing, even if they have to break the law to do so.

► Some countries have laws to protect whistle-blowers.

► Freedom of information laws can help whistle-blowers by bringing information on government wrongdoing to public scrutiny.

CHAPTER 7

The future for freedom of information

Although freedom of information legislation can be wide-ranging, it refers mainly to government departments and agencies. Campaigners point out that the economy is dominated by giant companies, yet we know very little about them as either consumers or citizens.

Opening the private sector up to freedom of information laws would face fierce opposition. Companies argue that they are already legally obliged to provide information to their shareholders and that their activities are overseen by regulatory bodies. They say that if they were expected to comply with freedom of information legislation, they would reveal valuable information to competitors and suppliers and this would put them at a commercial disadvantage. Honest companies, who supply information, would suffer, while dishonest companies, who give incorrect or incomplete information, would benefit.

Furthermore, companies in countries with freedom of information laws would be at a disadvantage compared to companies in countries without such laws, or where corruption was common. In response, some companies would move their operations overseas to avoid freedom of information laws and the government would lose valuable taxes and jobs.

In many countries governments use private companies to carry out government services. Most commonly, these are 'backroom functions' like collecting and processing data, but they may include direct services such as collecting and disposing of rubbish, maintaining roads, and running schools and health centres. Many people argue that private companies providing public services should be subject to freedom of information legislation, but others feel that this would place extra 'red tape' on hard-pressed companies (especially smaller companies) and discourage them from applying to work for governments.

However, many supporters of freedom of information feel that these arguments are a smokescreen that allows private sector companies to withhold valuable information from the public, media and regulators, and enables them to behave secretively and unethically.

The world of finance

Banks and other financial institutions have come under particular scrutiny since 2008 when the world financial system almost collapsed. Some banks were rescued from bankruptcy by government action; however the costs were high in both money and human terms and millions of people lost their jobs and homes. It appeared that some banks presented their shareholders with a rosy picture while huge financial and other problems were not disclosed. Other groups, such as private equity companies, do not have shareholders or regulators, and operate behind closed doors.

Would the situation have been avoided had banks been subject to freedom of information legislation? Campaigners believe that greater openness is vital if financial institutions are to be more trustworthy and stable. Others feel that freedom of information laws would not solve the problem because financial issues are so complex that even experts cannot understand them. They argue that better regulation and the ability of governments to take tough action are more important.

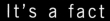

It's a fact

In 2015 the Scottish government announced a consultation on whether private companies and charities who had contracts to deliver services such as prisons, education and housing should be subject to Scotland's Freedom of Information Act. Many people supported the extension of the Act but some business leaders denounced the move as an extra cost for hard-pressed companies.

▼ The world financial system almost collapsed in September 2008, with investment bank Lehman Brothers filing for bankruptcy. Many campaigners say problems arose because banks and other financial institutions gave investors incomplete or inaccurate information, and that greater transparency is vital to protect investors and customers.

▲ A huge demonstration takes place in Tehran, Iran, as opposition supporters protest against rigged election results on 13 June 2009. Young demonstrators used mobile phones and digital cameras to bring information about the election and the violent crackdown on protesters to the world.

Global freedom of information

Information crosses country borders. This is part of the process of globalization – whereby the world is linked through trade networks, fast modern transport and electronic communication. Governments, businesses and legal systems are more entwined than ever before. The Internet allows users to access information from websites from all over the world and to send information and images through email and social networks.

Mobile phones and Skype link people worldwide and 24-hour television news channels transmit news as it happens. Information crosses from one website to another. If one government attempts to ban or limit information through legislation or a court order then the information may be easily accessible through the Internet.

Sometimes this has a huge political impact. For example, during the "Arab Spring" of early 2011 democracy protesters in Tunisia and Egypt used mobile phones to send messages and images about police and army brutality. In 2010 a group called WikiLeaks (see page 21) used an international network of computer servers to download hundreds of thousands of official but secret documents on American military activities in Afghanistan and Iraq and American diplomatic missions aboard. The material became available for public viewing and summaries were published in leading media despite angry protests from the US and other governments.

case study

Exposing company secrecy

Big companies can try to restrict media reporting by using the legal system. This was the case with Trafigura, an oil export company with a controversial record. In 2006 Trafigura disposed of toxic oil waste in the West African country of Ivory Coast, where it was much cheaper to do so than in Europe. The results were disastrous. A gas cloud hung over the city of Abjidan and thousands of people crowded hospitals with skin burns, damage to their eyes and lungs.

Trafigura commissioned a report on the situation from scientific experts. However, its findings were unwelcome and would be harmful to the company's reputation and the report remained secret. In 2009 when the *Guardian* newspaper in London wanted to summarise the report findings, Trafigura's lawyers served them with an injunction – a legal order barring them from publication. In addition, the lawyers asked for and received a 'super injunction' – a legal order stopping all mention of the original injunction. When an MP in the House of Commons asked questions about the injunction, the *Guardian* was told that it could not report the questions.

Instead, the paper published a front page story stating that it had been barred from reporting the proceeding of Parliament – a right established in the eighteenth century. The story caused outrage – and web-savvy investigators soon discovered the name of the company and the parliamentary questions. Within hours, information about the company, the report and the injunction was one of the top stories on Twitter. Soon there was so much information made public that the lawyers had to drop the injunctions and enable the media to report on the story.

Freedom of information today

Today over 100 countries have some form of freedom of information legislation, together with a system of access and a right of complaint and appeal. Other countries are in the process of adopting similar laws. In addition, there are many states and territories with their own freedom of information legislation, such as US and Australian states and Canadian provinces.

When freedom of information laws were first introduced they were the product of western democratic countries. From their beginnings in Scandinavia, then the US, they spread first to English-speaking and western European countries. From the 1990s, countries in eastern Europe, Asia and the Americas passed freedom of information laws as part of a wave of democratic reforms. The twenty-first century saw many more countries adopt freedom of information legislation.

It's a fact

When China enacted its national freedom of information law in May 2008, it wasn't surprising that many government agencies proved reluctant or obstructive in providing information. However there was a large and enthusiastic response of the public to exercise their new rights. Requests varied from individuals seeking personal files to questions on the cost and impact of huge projects such as the Three Gorges dam. The media regularly reports on cases and is actively educating the public on freedom of information issues.

▼ Nepal's radio journalists hold placards and march during a protest in Katmandu, Nepal, on June 1 2005. The banner reads 'Struggle to save freedom of radio' and the various placards also call for freedom of media.

They include developing countries like India and Bangladesh and countries like China who have limits on political activity. By 2015, 104 countries had passed freedom of information laws, with others updating previous laws to include new developments in information technologies.

However, there still are widespread problems even with laws in place. Often the legislation is defective and covers only some areas of government. Public servants may be unaware or untrained for their new responsibilities.

Delays are common and complaint and appeal procedures are complex and bureaucratic. However, the biggest single problem in nearly all countries seems to be that very few members of the public know about their rights and how to make use of freedom of information. As a result, in many cases the laws are unknown and little used (see table page 28).

The way forward

However, despite all the problems and pitfalls, in just fifty years, the principle of freedom of information has become widely accepted, both as an individual human right and as a responsibility of government to its citizens. Today the arguments are about how to apply the principle so that it works both for the government and the public. Should it be applied widely or narrowly? Who decides what information, if any, is to be withheld? How do we balance issues of public access against individual privacy? How do we deal with the ever-increasing amounts of information that are being generated by government? These are the questions that challenge us today and in the future.

viewpoints

'Today marks a new era of transparency and accountability in government. The reforms apply the principle that government information is a national resource – just like our water, our minerals and our beaches. Information is an asset for all to share in, wherever possible. It is not the possession of one agency or individual.'
Brendan O'Connor, Minister for Privacy and Freedom of Information, Australia, 1 November 2010

'After the Freedom of Information Act was passed in 1966, there were predictions by mournful government officials that there could be no more secrets – and yet, our bureaucrats quickly adapted, finding ways to keep things in the dark.'
James Mann, 'Keeping Secrets, even from WikiLeaks', CBS News, 30 November 2010

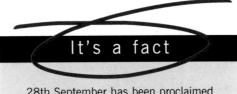

It's a fact

28th September has been proclaimed International Right to Know day to celebrate the right to freedom of information worldwide.

summary

▶ Private companies are not subject to freedom of information legislation, although some freedom of information campaigners feel they should be.

▶ The development of global communications through the Internet means that it is easier for information to cross country borders.

▶ Over 90 countries have introduced freedom of information legislation, and others are considering doing so.

Glossary

Accountable Responsible for one's actions.

Appeal A legal right to challenge a court ruling.

Archives An institution which catalogues and stores documents and other historic material.

Arms industry Companies making weapons for their own government or for sale overseas.

Bribery Criminally agreeing to give money to someone for favours, goods or services.

Bureaucratic Excessive rules and regulations, which are complex and unhelpful.

Cabinet A group of the most important ministers in a government.

Campaigning Activity aimed at changing public opinion or government policies.

Classified Kept secret.

Corruption Criminal activity, usually involving wrongly taking money for goods and services.

Democracy A country with a government elected by the people.

Disclosure Making something public.

Enron A giant energy company which went bankrupt in late 2001 after committing financial fraud on a gigantic scale. Post-Enron means after the fraud at Enron was exposed.

Exempt Not included.

Federal government The national or central government in a country divided into states or provinces.

Feudal Commonly used to mean old-fashioned and unhelpful.

FOIA Common abbreviation for Freedom of Information Act, the US federal freedom of information legislation.

Fraud Criminal activity, usually involving financial matters.

Freedom of information The right of a person to gain public access to government information, including policy statements, decisions, facts and statistics.

Legislation The details of a law.

Legitimate Proper, appropriate and lawful.

Lobbying Attempting to influence legislators on a particular issue.

Media Ways of conveying information and entertainment to the public, mainly through newspapers, magazines, television, radio and associated websites.

Memo An abbreviation of memorandum. A written message in business or diplomacy.

Penalised Punished.

Personal files Information on an individual, for example, medical or social security records.

Personal privacy The right for a person to keep their personal details from public access or general knowledge.

Private sector Business which are not part of government but which are owned by individuals or shareholders.

Procedures Agreed ways of doing something.

Proportionate Balanced, or done in such a way that the reaction matches the action.

Public servants People employed by the government; also called civil servants.

Public services Services such as health care, education and transport, run by the government.

Redacted A document has been presented in a censored format, where content has been removed or deleted.

Regulator A government agency, set up to oversee an activity or industry and ensure that it is run effectively, legally and safely.

Transparency Openness, resulting in a willingness to display information.

Twitter Electronic messaging, limited to 140 characters, sent via computers or mobile phones. A message is called a tweet.

Vendetta Campaign of revenge.

Watchdog A common name given to a regulatory body.

Whistle-blower A person who acts to reveal secret or hidden information and bring it to the public's attention.

Timeline

1766 Sweden adopts the world's first freedom of information law, the *Offentlighetsprincipe*, translated as the 'Principle of Publicity'.

1789 In France revolutionaries overthrow the despotic government and issue the Declaration of the Rights of Man and Citizens, one of the earliest human rights documents. Among its provisions, it declares that public servants should be accountable for their actions.

1881 Colombia passes a law ordering publicity of all official acts and documents.

1951 Freedom of information legislation introduced in Finland. In 1999, the law is revised and made stronger.

1966 The US passes its first freedom of information legislation which applies only to federal government agencies. The law was amended in 1996 to include forms of electronic information and updated again in 2009. Each US state and territory has its own freedom of information legislation.

1970 Denmark and Norway pass their first freedom of information legislation. Both are later replaced by stronger laws.

1976 Mexico amends Article 6 of its Constitution to include the right to freedom of information. In 2002, it passes a freedom of information law to put this right into effect.

1978 Freedom of information legislation introduced in France, which establishes a citizen's right to see any public document and an independent authority to oversee the process. A Freedom of Information law was also introduced in the Netherlands which was replaced by a stronger law in 1991.

1982 Australia adopts federal Freedom of information legislation, later followed by FOI laws at state level. In 2010, stronger federal FOI laws are introduced. In the same year, New Zealand also passes a Freedom of Information law.

1983 Canada adopts a Dominion (federal) Access to Information Act, together with a Privacy Act, the two laws are intended to complement and counterbalance each other, later followed by FOI laws at province level.

1985 Freedom of information legislation introduced in Greece.

1987 Freedom of information legislation introduced in Austria.

1990 Freedom of information legislation introduced in Italy.

1992 Freedom of information legislation introduced in Hungary, Spain and Ukraine.

1993 Article 32 of the Constitution of Belgium is amended to include rights to freedom of information. Freedom of information legislation is introduced in Kazakhstan and Portugal.

1994 Freedom of information legislation introduced in Belize and Greenland.

1995 Freedom of information legislation introduced in Hong Kong.

1996 Freedom of information legislation introduced in Iceland and Republic of Korea (South Korea).

1997 Freedom of information legislation introduced in Ireland (amended 2003), Thailand and Uzbekistan.

1998 Freedom of information legislation introduced in Israel and Latvia.

1999 Freedom of information legislation introduced in Albania, Czech Republic, Georgia, Liechtenstein, Japan, Trinidad and Tobago.

2000 Freedom of information laws introduced in Bulgaria, Estonia, Lithuania, Moldova, Slovakia, South Africa (a right of citizens to access government information was included in the new constitution of 1996), UK (the laws did not apply to Scotland which passed its own law in 2002).

2001 Freedom of information laws introduced in Bosnia-Herzegovina, Panama, Poland and Romania. The European Union also introduced freedom of information provisions to allow access to all documents produced by the European Parliament, Council and Commission.

2002 Freedom of information laws introduced in Angola, Jamaica, Pakistan, Scotland, Tajikistan, Zimbabwe.

2003 Freedom of information laws introduced in Argentina, Armenia, Croatia, Kosovo, Slovenia and Turkey.

2004 Freedom of information laws introduced in Switzerland, Dominican Republic, Ecuador, Faroe Islands and Serbia.

2005 Freedom of information legislation introduced in Azerbaijan, Germany (updated 2013), India (several Indian states had already introduced FOI laws), Montenegro, Republic of China (Taiwan) and Uganda.

2007 Freedom of information laws introduced in Jordan, Kyrgyzstan, Nepal and Nicaragua.

2008 China introduces 'Regulations on Open Government Information'.

2009 Freedom of information legislation introduced in Bangladesh, Chile, Guatemala, Iran, Russia and Uruguay.

2010 Freedom of information laws introduced in Indonesia and Liberia.

2011 Freedom of information laws introduced in Brazil, El Salvador, Hungary, Malta, Mongolia, Nigeria, Niger and Tunisia.

2012 Freedom of information laws introduced in Yemen.

2013 Freedom of information laws introduced in Guyana, Ivory Coast, Rwanda, Sierra Leone, South Sudan and Spain.

2014 Freedom of information laws introduced in Afghanistan, Maldives, Mozambique, Paraguay.

2016 USA celebrates 50 years of Freedom of Information Act. Sweden and Finland celebrate 250 years of the world's first Freedom of Information law.

* The dates indicate when freedom of information legislation passed into law, not when it came into effect, which could be several years later.

Further information

Books:

Global Questions: What are Human Rights?
Joseph Harris (Franklin Watts, 2010)

Ethical Debates: Privacy and Surveillance
Cath Senker (Wayland, 2011)

Websites:

http://www.cfoi.org.uk
A UK campaigning organisation, campaigning for freedom of information.

http://fightcorruption.wikidot.com
J.N. Jayashree's website – Fight Corruption Now.

http://www.freedominfo.org
News on Freedom of information worldwide.

http://www.sunshineingovernment.org
Sunshine in Government Initiative – US campaigning organisation aimed at opening up the process of government.

Index